THE US

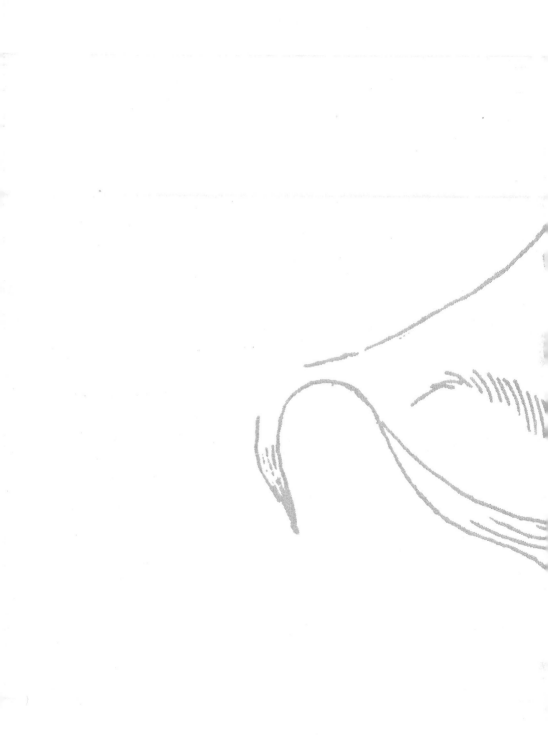

To Patrick, with unmatch... and admiration for your work. Hoping to see more of you. Best wishes, Joan

THE US

JOAN HOULIHAN

Joan Houlihan

May 16, 2010

Tupelo Press

North Adams, Massachusetts

The Us

Library of Congress Cataloging-in-Publication Data

Houlihan, Joan.
The us : poems / by Joan Houlihan. – 1st paperback ed.
     p.   cm.
ISBN 978-1-932195-77-4 (pbk. : alk. paper)
I. Title.
PS3608.O85545U8 2009
811'.6–DC22
2009017801

Cover and text designed in the fonts Electra and Lithos by Josef Beery.
Cover photograph: Neolithic pictographs in Cuevas de las Manos in Argentina.
The hand-drawn image that appears on the cover and title page is based on an
"upper paleolithic" drawing from the Altamira Cave in Spain.

Printed in the United States.
First paperback edition, September, 2009.
13 12 11 10 09   5 4 3 2 1

Tupelo Press
P.O. Box 1767, North Adams, Massachusetts 01247
Telephone: (413) 664–9611 / Fax: (413) 664–9711
editor@tupelopress.org / www.tupelopress.org

Tupelo Press is an award-winning independent literary press that publishes
fine fiction, non-fiction, and poetry in books that are a joy to hold as well as
read. Tupelo Press is a registered 501(c)3 non-profit organization, and we rely
on public support to carry out our mission of publishing extraordinary work
that may be outside the realm of the large commercial publishers. Financial
donations are welcome and are tax deductible.

Supported in part by an award from
the National Endowment for the Arts

NATIONAL
ENDOWMENT
FOR THE ARTS

for Eric

CONTENTS

PART III

Wherein the us continue their trek without ay & discover an isle.

PART IV

Wherein ay, she & brae hide in the forest then reunite with the us as they return from the isle and reach the mainland.

PART V

Wherein the injured ay is speechless & immobile & tended by the us.

ARGUMENT

A group of Primitive People travels over land & sea enduring cold & starvation; they sail to an Isle & live in harmony amidst Horse & Geese; a Strange Tragedy befalls them there; one who has stayed behind on the Mainland is captured by a group of Advanced People; he endures imprisonment & misfortune then escapes; he is reunited with his group when they return to the Mainland; an inexplicable Act of Violence changes all.

KITH & KIN

us   group of primitive people who speak as one

father   leader of the us

ay   son of father

brae   second son of father & g'wen; brother of ay

g'wen   wife of father; mother of ay & brae

sen   wise female elder; conjurer

thems   group of advanced people who would enslave the us

she   one of the thems; nursemaid of brae

greb   one of the us who is sly & dangerous

PART I

Wherein the us are portrayed in everyday life.

Us nest fine

Us nest fine a weather long
between the heat of kin
the least of us in huts built round with stones.
A sky-hole takes the cook-smoke through.

Ice-taught, bit by sun's low arc,
rock-tall, quiet as a smoke
ours father goes before us
knows what moves and is a fur.

It takes the scare of born
and dawn shook down,
a work of teeth and softening
that marks the least of us, and beast, as one,
makes the broth go sweet
and fat, and under pelt
warms all the count of us
and more who will be born.

Morning, and as sun is born

Morning, and as sun is born from dark
ours father took the track to where
the red deer ran except one stood
great-headed, tall,
of a size and look to put in mind
the reach of what us were and came to be
and how us were the smaller,

What formed hims elk-head
godly, as from an inner body,
bone-branched, notched and wide
spread and sprouted out and up
and him on a standing, watchful
and seen, ran the forest,
head-struck and stuck
between the trees.

Ours stick sharp for the kill
lifted high, in and in, and from hims throat
a groan went, leg bent,
knelt, then all of him were loosed and spread
in large and steaming breath,
ours stick-holes streaming red.

A *kind of cold*

A kind of cold and moon rise
changed the air and told us
coming dark. Us cut the elk
apart — hoofs tossed —
and by antlers pulled
hims head, eyes alive.

Hail the kill and all it bring!

Ours father, bowed and slow, behind,
would point us on, not keep to him.

As fruit begins by seed and shows itself in time
the gleam that sees from night grew in.

Hail, hail!

The trunk ran red. Moon lit the smear
dragged on snow.

Grown unfit

The father is ill.

Grown unfit to sit or eat,
tinged with ice, not quiet —
a labor, us to raise and carry
down to bed.

Him may have worn a pelt,
looked a way us can't remember
before the last bolt shot.

Wanting talk, him takes the smooth food
cold, and us make out the day
of hims away, putting him to thought.

*A deathwatch
begins.*

Nowhere rue, but something simple, old.
Him would leave us nothing but a god.

Beside the bed

Beside the bed us hailed and poked
hims length with sticks. Were him?
Not eye us round or shout.

Boldened, us came close and looked full on.
The fire inside hims eye were down.

On beard and lip, a fly would stop
then up and stop again. Hims time.

The only wind-hole knocked against
with blown and snowy branch
put us quiet and in mind
of ours beyond and all the good in that.

No more master in the home.
Us foraged in the nooks for what him bided with.
What kept him long were empty and upturned.
Hims last of meat us took and tore.

Hims g'wen sat on the floor and would not eat.

Then, as always would,
us lifted, put him to the pyre,
lit fire and went.

And all were done but what
hims g'wen would watch.

*By law, the
father's body
must be
burned.*

Many days, and then the fire, us raked it low
and a fingerbone found for the sen
to spend in hers powders and sayings,
to save us from him
who are not with us now.

When the catalpa

The father's death & spring's omens give command to go.

When the catalpa dangled
little blackened elbows
each to be struck with a beak
were right for us to go.

And the sen made us a powder
mixt of father and water
to sprinkle on an ill-turned brae or
onto a barren belly, or

The us capture the father's spirit in the sen's powder.

rub in ours hands when
ours homes come down
and only a small fire warms.

Standing white

Standing white at morning
ash along hers forehead
under the catalpa —
us put to hims g'wen a bowl.

And after the flight of hims ashes
cold light knocked along the trees
and her would not be left
but kept to us, mute and straight,
behind and far apart.
Us walked, would not look back.

*By law the
mourning
g'wen must
stay behind,
but she
follows the
group.*

Bare evening ate

Bare evening ate into ours heat
and builded winter up. Gone
from him, the g'wen kept on:
Another to be born!
and put a show of eating
to hers mouth,

Broth were measured out
and crustings of a count
that did not count her in.

*The g'wen is
pregnant &
cannot keep up.*

In days hers step not strong
made her slow and drag.
The us kept on. Ay went back.

Small noise and in the air
hers hand went up and weak.
Hers eye went strange, held onto mine.

Ay am hers son
and would not leave her colding.

PART II

Wherein the brae is born, g'wen dies & ay is made captive of thems.

And g'wen were smaller

And g'wen were smaller then, as smoke is
from the last, hearing the us go far.
Ay drag a kindle where she lay.
Her would not stir, lay colder,
letting snow be on her.

Ay builded fire from what ay broke,
broke a crust for her.
Fire-tip waved and then the deeper stroke
took in. Its pieces blew up bright and
hung on air.

What hid or stepped between the trees
ay could not see.

Ay lay beside the fire.
Hers noise went in the air.

*The g'wen begins
her labor.*

Hers head went side to side

Hers head went side to side and groans
went round the wood, more
and hard against
what would be born.

What had a hold in her came loose,
alive and small to grip — the brae.
Ay took and wrapped in a torn-off cloth
to put it safe.

Hard awake and brae

Hard awake and brae had noise
full out for food.
Ay put him to the milk of her.
It would not flow.
She turned hers face away.

What filled hers throat were crackles
as a burning tosses high
then calls its fire down.
Ay bent to make her close.

*The son says
goodbye to his
mother.*

What lit her long, hers life inside,
were swerved and spilled and blown
then came back quiet to hers ground.

Why so noiseful

Why so noiseful, brae?
Can you give in voice so long?
You are a face and seeing small from it.
You are a mouth and wanting big for milk.
You are a carry.
How can ay make care for you?

Brae, stay here, the branch

Brae, stay here, the branch and leaf
a shield of sun, moss, a bed
and every bird a guard.

Am low and fast
to town, the plumes of smoke,
thems tending ground
and putting cow to milk —
to spy thems first,
steal from thems a kind
by smearing on mine face some dirt
and stumbling like one lost:

Oh, ay's a gone one here
not knowing where ay am —

Ay show the brae, taking thems
to where him lay.

What never were mine

*Ay hands the brae
to thems for care &
surrenders himself.*

What never were mine, ay gave
to thems, a small in the cloth
of mine father's g'wen — you, brae.
Taken to another hand
you cry but nothing know.
Ay stand in thems town with no want
to go and nowhere are mine kin.
Brae, you are taken for care
and ay belong to thems.

Put with the odd

Put with the odd, no kind or ilk
and nowhere to cling
or a given place, no track
to be on and follow,
a torn-out one, ay am shown the ground
to harrow and rake and flower a grain
for mouths ay had no talk with.

Thrown wide of sky, what goes on with no end,
ay am put to eyes that spy for a kill,
to plants that prick or poison, to animals after a gnaw.

No walking without a prod, no sleeping without a shout,
thems look up close: *what are ye? where from?*
what use are ye given? what tongue?
and mine own talk closed inside.

Tied to each other, foot to foot,   *Ay is put to work*
by loops of hemp, and mine   *in the field with*
give out sore at sun-fall.   *other captives.*

Ay see brae on the back of a she,
and she in the field as hard.

Had labor and more

Had labor and more: gnarl and beard, close to the sun and shiver.
Had dirt and hole, hand-hurt and plow, cut, bend and dig.
Had days and no end.
Had kneel. Had burn. Had sore and stings and many.
Had keep of the tongue, no kin.
Had stone-mouth, suffer and weather.
Had ay, and ay alone.

At night a milk-bowl

At night a milk-bowl,
soaking crust, thems give
so not to waste the meat.
Ay eat beside a wind-hole, seeing
sky to where ay could not see.
Thems slide out a box
the size of lying down
and told with a hand—
here—go inside.
Ay fit to it, then on top
thems set a lid for sleep.

*Ay sleeps in a
narrow box.*

Down low in fields

Down low in fields ay saw how cow and sheep went mild in sun's small place, gave to shade thems rest. Were such a way ay and other captives walked from field to hut, ours footing sore and dragging, waked in dark to walk and turned in dark to walk again with sacks of picking, grains to set in hollowed stones and crush. And bread were made by g'wens and smallers, put on pallets to a heat, and gave off soft and steaming blocks, and crustings, some, were tossed. And all were colder, holding talk, kept to a fire, made a circle of backs, and ay crept to catch heat from between.

Days and days again

Days and days again a rain
seeped into ditch and dirt to stay.
Meats were flyblown, taking taint.
Shaked out, drawn down, loose in the skin,
hog and cow, sheep and fowl
bled black and brayed to blue —
wide-eyed and the light gone through.

A contagion is spread.

From meat thems went

Eating the meat of
sick animals infects
the townspeople.

From meat thems went to stagger,
blotch and swell.
Some at plow let go
to lie in sweat and cold
and some not home
when night came down.

Arose to lower talk

Arose to lower talk around the bed
of one drawn down
as from a gutted candle snuffed
a pour of smoke.

Thems stood and looked at him
who emptied out. Hims g'wen did not go
quiet to the floor but tore hers cloth and wept.
Thems sen spent a saying, big with noise,
and not the way of ours.

Then came a loudening at the door.
Ay kept to mine corner, small
and put in mind ours father,
how hims death were done.

*Ay watches
the death of
thems leader ...*

Morning crept along the wall.
Thems lift him out.
Through a wind-hole ay saw a wood-pile,
bodies dragged and twisted on top.

Thems lay and stank.
A fiery cloth were put
and flame ran like a teasing brae
to peep from here and there.

Beyond that flare stood her who gave
hers milk. In hers arms, the brae.

*... then sees the
brae with his
nursemaid in
the crowd.*

A smoke struck high

A smoke struck high on night's half-light
and under, lowing flame. Captives wandered
loose, unspied, and piles of half-burned lay,
some ash, some char, some
ragged holes felt through by fire,
and some the face alone.

*In the
confusion,
prisoners
escape.*

In going, there were none to say
come back! She and brae had nothing
but to come to mine hand.

Us walked past cows
with hides crawled over,

*Ay escapes
with the brae
& nursemaid.*

past horses splayed and swole.

From dirt, a stir

From dirt, a stir put forth its mix, smell
of weed and green-held bud, deep cups
sweet and sharp. Warmer started day.
Sun lay wider where us walked.

And ay had seeing out to hers — long cloth tied
with hemp, of smaller head than ay, and that head bent
to sounds from brae, hers hair a gleam-fall over him,
the weaker, full of noise for her and lifting up.

And ay would turn to watch the smoke
go high in thin and thinner twist
the way the sun must bring its burning home.

PART III

Wherein the us continue their trek without ay
& discover an isle.

Froze by winter blast

Froze by winter blast
us could not grip on meat or crust,
ours fingers blackened down to all the hand.

And many fell that time
and so were fewer count of us
coming into weather, loosened snow,
water falling down around the stones.

Us heard command in that.

Rose again, the light, and rooted things crept out,
greenly took up spots between the snow.
What good there were for us
showed in starrys round the moon.

By roar and rush and smell of brine
us found the sea and stood along.

Sen's scatter-sticks and wobble-stones
gave command to go by boat
and find by water, home.

By harshening light

By harshening light and blue,
wave-washed on a plank
that creaked and knocked,
so cold the bread were froze,
us huddled, clung to each.

No ground to put us
only water with no end.
Us hove the dead ones in.

Two moons and more
from casting out
came loud against the side
caught in a notch of rock
sun wide on its face, an isle.

Where us stept

Where us stept a water sprung
to leaf and green and goose crept round
and eyed us, with a soft *grog, grog*
and a nodding
each one big as a swollen dove
with a hatching spot on the breast.

Us saw the speckled egg
unhidden for the taking.

Then horses low and red
came slow for us to ride
neck outstretched for hands,
eye cast down and soft
and nuzzled forth and bent for us to climb.

Fire at night closed us round
with creatures us once tamed or killed
and now would live among.

From branch shaked out

From branch shaked out and speckled egg,
us made new eating, not to harm
the ones of hoof and horn
and ground were dug and seeded
taking those to plow who were ours tame.

The us respect the animals, cultivate the land.

Night and day, day and night,
sun and rain took up the work
and gave a take of all that fruited
ripe and sweet from green.

Us lived, and us of all, as to a light
and drinking from the sun.
Night kept us as would a pelt
of highest fur, the stars its eyes around.

When one who eats

When one who eats what comes
from dirt or drops from trees
all with little pulp to wring
or boils to make a bitter drink —
him would have a fat, a smell,
a flesh that calls a tooth to it, tugs easy from the bone —
that one, a greb, would put hims mouth on meat
not bend to scrape for root or seed.
Him waits near horse until it grazes, strays,
lifts its head to gaze at him, and trust.

*One of the us,
a greb, desires
meat.*

Days, and the sea turned windward

Days, and the sea turned windward.
Blown-down grasses bowed.
A creaking strap and plow turned dirt.
Hoof chuffed and chuffed against.

Were kindred, low and gentle horse,
hims ears tipped back for a word,
hims mane shaked down in a water-fall
shined all over with reddened gold.

When found him under

When found him under fly-buzz,
killed in a field and bled,
us stood in a small way looking
at hide and muscle tore,
the large-lidded eye gone wide.

Hair lifted, parts of fur stirred here
or there like grass,
no feel of sky or dirt or ant
that walked along hims brow.
What made him horse were gone.

The killing of
a horse stuns
the us.

Then early day

Then early day, a small red horse
comes onto shore
lying on hims side, spread strange.

Sea cleans and licks him,
churning down, roots
in holes and narrow parts
for what were horse.

Late, awake, and few, us crept
to have an eye on things by dark.
The sen stirs fire, hers stick
makes wider rings around
the leaning of hims bones.

The sen speaks
her spell over the
horse's body &
conjures its spirit.

Hers telling, close and not for us,
hers seeing past the rim of fire,
embers floating up — all
for a shape that tossed in sea,
runs the sea-top, makes a horse.

Not for the plow

Not for the plow when us went to call
do many come, only some
with lowered head.

Thems sickened to us. All the light went out
inside thems coats. And in the strap not strong
or quickly stepped, but slow
with only half a planting down.

*The horses fear
the us & will
not work.*

Waked in deeper night us heard
the horses' sound of hurt.

Waked by wind, sea talk

Waked by wind, sea-talk, sound of a hurt horse walking,
us kept to the lying and lower, wound into a cover, knees tucked up.

As it shrilled on the cliff, clopped the rocks, stopped at ours door then passed,
us crept to the wind-holes, spied through cracks, eye to the dark, saw the bent-

down walk, how it stopped at a hut, lifted its head and went in.
Morning, that hut, smoke-dead, had a quiet spread out from the wind-holes

and us knew to leave it alone. Sen would enter and speak for what were took:
food-holes emptied, clothing tore, ours kindred stamped and killed.

Carried heavy and swaying, holding fast to arms and legs, us hove ours dead
over the cliff, down to where it lived.

Shaked later in sleep by wind crying up and sea as it fought the rocks, us lay
awake in dark, fearing to turn or talk.

Strapped to plow

Strapped to plow, us pulled a shallow rut.
What green grew up were took by beak
or snuck away by rat.

Us made a scare of stick and cloth.
Birds came down and sat along its arms
to watch us work.

Then us went round the coast
on foot, taking speckled eggs
and calling goose.
From trust, they came.
Us lay their necks along a rock.

Birds in quiver for a warmer place
turned a line against the sky and went.

Eaten soft by water

*The us go back
to their boat &
prepare for a
return voyage to
the mainland.*

Eaten soft by water and salt
tucked in a sea-cloth of weed
half on its side like an animal down —

closer, ours boards gone wavy and sprung,
skittered with crab, crawled with rat
and a walk on deck struck crackles of shell.
A coating of creature stuck to the planks.

Then gave a small eating hand to hand
as over ours heads cloth flapped, a tatter
near undone.

Who of us took to clearing weed
who of us downed the tatter to mend
who of us put a hand to wood
who of us dug it from sand —

who of us mattered none
only that it were done.

PART IV

Wherein ay, she & brae hide in the forest then reunite with the us as they return from the isle and reach the mainland.

Curling, winding, stem

Curling, winding, stem and spear
green-held, weighed with pod.
A lock of branches high and twined
spread leafs as lids against the light
and deep in age, the trees
would keep us hid.

Brae's arms loosened from hers neck
and him were lain in a greeny dent.
She opened hers cloth of fruit and seed.
Hers look came out to mine.

*The three
escapees find
peace in the
forest.*

Sun were simple, birds had talk.
Night came on a reddened horse,
hoofs tossed sparks to strike the dark.

And ay would wake and feel the turn
of grass, hear a coming tap
along the trunks and feel the air
along mine face, then see the two
with bodies curled together,
sleeping small in larger
shadows like a water.
Quieted, ay curled around them both.

Weather brought redder berries

Weather brought redder berries, sweet
still tucked in nut and seed.
Ours hut were raised by lifting stone
on stone, and she and the brae would labor.

Ay made a stick sharp for hunt, a snare to trap,
crept soft to the boar to hide
and watch. Ours days would pass.

*The ay, the
nursemaid &
the brae make
camp in the
forest.*

And soon ay went far
and came to a shore, went far
and came to the sea.

Who put there, water

Who put there, water
built with light inside, pushed
and thrust it high or lay
it down and tame?

What had water done
to be a captive of sky?
And why that speck
to ride its back
not slapped to splinter
taken down
into the place water keeps to eat?

Ay see that speck come
closer every wave.

*His reverie at
the sea's edge...*

*...becomes
curiosity about
the ship in the
distance.*

Against the sky

Against the sky cloth hung.
Rend and strip took little billow from the wind.
Swells brought it to mine shore. Ay called out
for what were there but rot and rat.

*Ay sees what
looks like an
empty vessel
coming to shore.*

The us came slowly

The us came slowly off, red-bearded,
burnt to hues of dirt, sack and bundle open,
dragged in loose and odd-kept ways, wrapped
in pelt that fell to shreds or did not cover every skin
but left some part for weather.

Ay saw how weak the us, and swayed,
how smallers carried braes
with low and keen-like pitch.

One by one each comes
to stand and look at ay,
and sen to lay her hand.
Ay bent mine head to that.

The us tell
of their
misfortunes
on the isle.

Some tell how horse
were wronged and killed for meat,
fled the plow and wandered hurt, away.

Others pulled the boat to rest
and took what food were left.
With them came the greb.

Creb and ay were fast to rise

Greb and ay were fast to rise at day,
strike the flint for a gleam
and sharp ours sticks.

*Greb is eager to
hunt with ay.*
In quiet us two fit our walk
to wild and halfway seen
bristle-boar through trees
and toward us snorting,
tooth curved up and sharp
wide snout black and wet.

With shouts and charging stuck him.
The blood went full and bright.

Thrusting up, him staggered blind,
went down. Greb stuck him then, mouth to end
and hefted on a stick us took the meat,
wakened others for a take.

Taste of cold came in

Taste of cold came in, meat
were stored, ours hunt were done.
Greb would kill the more —
spent another, streaming red.
Him called to me to see it end.

And when grebs arm raised
with a rock
him turned to crack it down — not on the boar —
on ay.
Ay heard him call to the us:

*Ay is taken
by surprise
by greb's
attack.*

Him falls!

Carried home by the us and cold,
ay flowed mine living out.

PART V

*Wherein the injured ay is speechless &
immobile & tended by the us.*

Rain made me here

Rain made me here. What would speak me,
have a noise? Even bird would
fold and pleat then leaf-stirred make its cry
and go. How could winter matter, touched rattling
to a tree, holding white and close
another sleep? Ay could not tell.
Ay came back simple, milded, felled.

*Ay contemplates
his state.*

Such comfort as were

Such comfort as were kindled —
sidelong, drawn, quick to the eye —
she and brae gave, work and talk
around the quiet that were ay
and watched for a caring or sign of wrong
not put as strange, aside,
but made as the day were, lain
at the hearth, so all would stoop to tend.
Would speak? ay heard, and quieted
mine eye and this us took for sleep.

Crawls on mine cloth

Crawls on mine cloth, a fret
of feet—stops, rubs quick
hims hands—then up, leans in,
hims eye comes near, and every hair,
then nose, a turning here
and there, then down to scat the floor.
Ay would lift mine hand and voice
to see him turn again.

A mouse
sparks the ay's
desire to move
& speak.

Day broke sky

Day broke sky to snow,
shifted track of boar.
Mine own path sifted, blown.

And brae came close
to tilt mine head
so ay could better see
and put hims hand along the spot
greb struck.

From all ay were before, in quiet
and as winter spent its cold,
the us forgot, except the brae
who came to tip the bowl.

To this cold

To this cold, no bird, no wood
with odors of burning
and all that lived showed its born

and rising. What could be killed
spoke of dying.
Autumn softened the cut,
spread low sounds in the field.

When hurt stops the mouth
what talks on? From what branch
a leaf, to gleam the eye?

When ay remember
what took me low —! No.
Ay died. Look —
the long grass is old with snow.

In spring ay am

In spring ay am taken out
to warm and dampening green.
Us toss some leavings near:
cloth ate by weather and tore,
handfuls of hair broke from pelts,
hemp rope with rot from damp.
All made us lighter for going.

And frost put its net on grass
for sun to lay down morning.

Greb came in close
to mine eye, and ay told *raise*
to mine hand. It raised.
Ay told *show* to mine finger. It pointed.

Were him. Were him. Ay told, but could not say.
And him stood quiet, far.

*Ay attempts
to expose the
greb.*

Lifted like a brae

Lifted like a brae, soft-turned by hands,
murmured on, wrapped in cloth, ay were
still. The us made a shade to lay me down.

Fanned and fed the sweet of fruit and nut,
broth of younger kill, ay were a wait,
mine father's son, and tended.

And from every show ay made, the us
took a telling —
how mine finger moved to point a snow,
how mine eye blinked rain.

*Ay is closely
watched &
revered.*

Rubbed and blowed on, covered
with cloth, and sen made a small of me
from clay, stuck it on a branch to dry.

She raised it at morning, spent a saying.
And again at evening when the us lay down
and fire ate its wood then went under
to sleep in a cover of crumble,
speckles of light going out.

And ay heard them whisper mine power
as ay lay in swaddle, alive, unable.

Ay were alive

Ay were alive, a sky were mine
cracked cold and furred along the hill.

On thresh of limb and stem
rough-made with leaf-
crush, moss, ay were a carry.

Hurried with a brush and squeak
on crusted snow none looked down
to where ay lay and did not speak.

Put by at camp, ay felt a break,
alone. Ay were struck deep.

*The us are
resigned to
moving again.*

The us had lost a want to build against
the cold and stay. The only watchful
fire were glint then spent
and us went on. Ay saw tops of trees, some melt
from snow, a quake of shaggy branch and gold
between the leaf. The us had broke. Ay felt the fault.

ACKNOWLEDGMENTS

Boston Review
"From branch shaked out"
"Where us stepped"

Fulcrum
"Morning, and as dark"
"A kind of cold"
"Grown unfit"

*Harvard Divinity
Bulletin*
"Froze by winter blast"
"Ay were alive"
"A cloth bled high"

*The Book of Irish-
American Poetry*
(University of Notre Dame
Press, 2007)
"Waked by wind, sea talk"

*Wild Apples:
a journal of nature,
art, and inquiry*
"From dirt, a stir"
"Strapped to plow"

I am deeply grateful to my husband, Eric Howlett, who accompanied me on this strange journey, providing encouragement and clear-sightedness along the way, and to those friends and colleagues who helped in shaping the early stages of the manuscript — Adam Dressler, for his whip-smart readings, and Susan Zilenski, for her intelligence and encouragement — and to Ilya Kaminsky for his helpful comments on the later manuscript. Thanks, truly, to Jeffrey Levine, who made this all finally real, and to Jim Schley for helping bring it into the world. I am grateful to Fred Marchant for his humanity and insight and to Steven Cramer for his unabashed support of this work. I also thank the late Reginald Shepherd for his greatly missed love and influence.

And night, ay saw him

And night, ay saw him, hoof and head,
antlers branching, trunk bled out
soaking hill and sky —
ours father come as never killed, as tall
and with a look that bathed me warm.

It were not death, a carry in mine chest
of what were spent and spilled,
that made of blood another shape
and scent, a fire, a want to blaze,
a rage that tipped and branched
to where the sun could make it strong.

And brae would spoon the broth,
make talk between us
where mine own had gone,
as sounding saved by water,
rivered in its mouth
when saving ay had none
and all mine days were silt
and through the hand.